Bagels from S__

Homemade Recipes for Making and Enjoying
Tasty Bagels at Home

BY

Alex Aton

- ■ -■-■-■-■-■-■-■-■-■-■-■-■-■-■

Licensing Information

It is strictly prohibited to engage in any commercial or non-commercial activity related to the content of this book without the explicit permission of the author. This includes, but is not limited to, selling, publishing, printing, copying, disseminating, or distributing the content in any form or medium. The author holds exclusive rights to the content and reserves the right to take legal action against any unauthorized usage.

If you have obtained an illegal copy of this book, please delete it immediately and obtain a legal version. Purchasing a legal version of this book supports the author's hard work and dedication in creating the content.

However, the author does not take responsibility for any actions taken by the reader based on the information provided in the book. The content is intended solely as an informational tool and the author has taken all necessary steps to ensure its accuracy. However, as with any information source, caution must be exercised when taking any steps based on the content of this book. It is advisable to seek professional guidance before taking any significant actions based on the information provided in this book.

- ■ - ■ - ■ - ■ - ■ - ■ - ■ - ■ - ■ - ■ - ■ - ■ - ■

Table of Contents

Introduction... 6

Classic Bagels 8

   1. Homemade Bagels.. 9

   2. Bagel Bonanza..12

   3. Sesame Seed Bagels 15

   4. Cinnamon Raisin Bagels....................................18

   5. Autumn Spice Bagels.......................................21

   6. Poppy Seed Bagels 24

   7. Garlicky Bagel Rings.......................................27

   8. Whole Wheat Bagels 31

   9. Blueberry Bagels 34

   10. Onion Bagels 37

Savory Bagel Sandwiches...................................40

   11. Steak and Egg Bagel Sandwich.......................41

   12. Sunrise Bagel Sandwich.................................44

13. Turkey Avocado Bagel Bomb 47

14. Eggy Bagel Stack 50

15. Veggie Bagel Bonanza 53

16. Chicken Salad Bagel Supreme 56

17. Smoked Salmon Bagel Stack 59

18. Honey Apple Bagel Bonanza 62

19. Toasted Bagel Delight 65

20. Tuna Twist Bagel Bonanza 68

Sweet Bagel Treats 70

21. Chocolate Chip Bagels 71

22. Sweet Sunrise Bagel 74

23. Strawberry Cream Cheese Bagel Bliss 77

24. Bagel French Toast Surprise 79

25. Bagel with Peanut Butter and Jelly 82

36. Peachy Cream Bagel Bliss 85

27. Blueberry Bagel Bliss 87

28. Sweet & Savory Bagel Stack 90

29. Blueberry Bliss Bagel 93

30. Apple Cinnamon Bagel...96

Conclusion..98

My Words 100

Introduction

Welcome to the world of homemade bagels! This cookbook is your guide to making delicious, New York-style bagels right in your own kitchen. We've gathered a collection of recipes that cover everything from classic plain bagels to creative flavored varieties and tasty bagel sandwiches.

Bagels have been a beloved breakfast staple for generations, and now you can learn the secrets to making them at home. Our recipes are easy to follow and use simple ingredients you can find in any grocery store. Whether you're a beginner baker or an experienced cook, you'll find these recipes approachable and fun to make.

In this book, you'll learn the basic techniques for mixing, shaping, and boiling bagels to get that perfect chewy texture and golden crust. We'll show you how to make traditional favorites like sesame and poppy seed bagels, as well as more unique flavors like blueberry and pumpkin spice.

But we don't stop at just bagels. We've also included a variety of sandwich recipes that showcase how versatile bagels can be. From hearty breakfast sandwiches to light lunch options and even sweet treats, you'll find plenty of ideas to enjoy your homemade bagels.

Each recipe comes with helpful tips and variations, so you can customize your bagels to your liking. We've also included information on storing and freezing bagels, so you can always have fresh bagels on hand.

Get ready to fill your home with the irresistible aroma of freshly baked bagels. Let's start baking!

Classic Bagels

1. Homemade Bagels

These bagels are a New York classic, now made easy at home. They're chewy, golden, and perfect for breakfast or snacks. With just a few ingredients, you'll make bagels that rival any bakery. Once you try these, store-bought just won't cut it anymore.

Preparation Time: 2 hours 30 minutes

Serving size: 12 bagels

Ingredients:

For the Bagels:

- 5&3/4 cups all-purpose flour
- 2&1/4 cups warm water
- 2&1/4 teaspoons sea salt
- 4 teaspoons honey
- 1 tablespoon active dry yeast (or instant yeast)

For Boiling:

- 10 cups water
- 1/4 cup honey

For the Egg Wash:

- 2 tablespoons water
- 1 egg

Instructions:

a. Mix water, honey, and yeast in a cup. Let it sit for 5 minutes.
b. In a big bowl, mix flour and salt.
c. Add yeast mix to flour. Stir until dough forms.
d. Knead dough on a floured surface for 10-15 turns.

e. Put dough in a bowl, cover with plastic. Let rise 60-90 minutes.

f. After rising, put dough on the work surface.

g. Start water boiling with honey. Turn heat to medium.

h. Heat oven to 425°F. Line 2 baking sheets with parchment.

i. Cut dough into 12 pieces. Roll each into a ball.

j. Make holes in balls with fingers. Stretch to form bagel shape.

k. Let shaped bagels rest for 5 minutes.

l. Boil bagels 1-2 at a time, 1.5-2 minutes per side.

m. Put boiled bagels on baking sheets.

n. Mix egg and water. Brush on bagel tops.

o. Bake for 15-18 minutes until golden brown.

p. Cool a bit, then move to the wire rack.

q. Enjoy with cream cheese or your favorite topping!

Special Notes:

- For extra flavor, add 1 tablespoon of malt syrup to the boiling water. It gives bagels a subtle, sweet taste.
- Try sprinkling sesame seeds, poppy seeds, or everything bagel seasoning on top right after the egg wash for variety.

2. Bagel Bonanza

These bagels are a New York staple that's taken over the world. They're chewy, tasty, and perfect for breakfast or lunch. With a crispy outside and soft inside, they're topped with a mix of seeds and spices. You'll love making these at home - they're easier than you think!

Preparation Time: 2 hours 20 minutes

Serving size: 15 bagels

Ingredients:

- 4&1/2 – 5&1/2 cups all-purpose flour
- 2 packets (1/4 oz each) active dry yeast
- 2 cups warm water
- 2 tablespoons honey
- 1 teaspoon salt
- 1 tablespoon brown sugar
- 2 tablespoons everything bagel seasoning

Instructions:

a. Mix warm water, yeast, and honey in a big bowl. Wait until it gets foamy.

b. Add salt and 4 cups of flour. Mix well. Keep adding flour bit by bit until the dough isn't sticky. You might use about 5 cups total.

c. Knead the dough until it's stretchy. Put it in a greased bowl and let it grow for an hour.

d. Punch the dough down. Cut it into 15 pieces, about 3 oz each. Roll each piece into a ball and put them on a greased baking sheet. Cover and wait 30 minutes.

e. Make a hole in the middle of each ball to form a bagel shape.

f. Heat your oven to 400°F. Boil water in a big pot and add brown sugar.

g. Cook the bagels in the water for 2 minutes, flip, then 30 seconds more. Take them out and put them back on the baking sheet.

h. Sprinkle everything bagel seasoning on top.

i. Bake for 28-35 minutes until they're golden brown. Let them cool before you cut and eat them.

Special Notes:

- For extra chewy bagels, let the shaped dough sit in the fridge overnight before boiling and baking.
- Try adding a tablespoon of barley malt syrup to the boiling water for a more authentic New York bagel flavor and color.

3. Sesame Seed Bagels

These sesame seed bagels are a New York breakfast staple. They're chewy, crusty, and loaded with nutty sesame flavor. People love them for their satisfying texture and versatility. Whether you slather them with cream cheese or pile on some lox, these bagels will start your day right.

Preparation Time: 2 hours 50 minutes

Serving Size: 8 Bagels

Ingredients:

- 3&1/3 cups bread flour
- 1&1/3 cups lukewarm water
- 1 tablespoon white sugar
- 2 tablespoons olive oil or vegetable oil 2 teaspoons instant yeast
- 1 tablespoon barley malt syrup (or molasses / honey)
- 1&1/2 teaspoons fine salt
- 1 teaspoon baking soda (for water bath)
- Black & white sesame seeds, to taste

Instructions:

a. Mix water, sugar, and yeast in a bowl. Wait 10 minutes until it's bubbly.
b. Add oil and syrup. Then mix in flour and salt. Knead with a stand mixer for 8-10 minutes until stretchy.
c. Cover and let rise for 1.5 hours in a warm spot.
d. Punch down dough and cut into 8 pieces.
e. Form each piece into a ball and poke a hole in the center to create a bagel shape.
f. Put half the bagels in the fridge while you work on the others.
g. Heat oven to 350°F. Boil water with baking soda in a pot.
h. Boil each bagel for 30-60 seconds per side. Let cool for a minute.

i. Dip in sesame seeds, then bake for 20-22 minutes until golden.

j. Repeat with the second batch.

Special Notes:

- For extra-chewy bagels, let the shaped dough rest in the fridge overnight before boiling and baking.
- Try mixing in some dried onion flakes or garlic powder into the dough for a flavor twist.

4. Cinnamon Raisin Bagels

Cinnamon Raisin Bagels are a hit breakfast item from New York. They're loved for their sweet and spicy taste. These bagels mix chewy dough with plump raisins and warm cinnamon. They're great toasted with butter or cream cheese. You'll want to make these often!

Preparation Time: 2 hours 30 minutes

Serving Size: 12 bagels

Ingredients:

For the Bagels:

- 5&3/4 cups all-purpose flour
- 2&1/4 cups warm water
- 1/2 cup raisins
- 4 teaspoons honey
- 2&1/4 teaspoons sea salt
- 2 teaspoons ground cinnamon
- 2 tablespoons raw sugar (or brown sugar)
- 1 tablespoon active dry yeast (or instant yeast)

For Boiling:

- 10 cups water
- 1/4 cup honey

For the Egg Wash:

- 1 egg
- 2 tablespoons water

Instructions:

a. Mix water, honey, and yeast in a cup. Let it sit for 5 minutes.

b.   In a big bowl, mix flour, salt, cinnamon, sugar, and raisins.

c.   Add yeast mix to flour mix. Stir until dough forms.

d.   Knead dough on a floured surface for 10-15 times.

e.   Put dough in a bowl, cover with plastic. Let rise for 60-90 minutes.

f.   After rising, put dough on the work surface.

g.   Start boiling water and honey in a pot.

h.   Heat oven to 425°F. Line 2 baking sheets with parchment.

i.   Cut dough into 12 pieces. Roll each into a ball.

j.   Make a hole in each ball with your fingers. Stretch to form bagel shape.

k.   Let bagels rest for 5 minutes.

l.   Boil bagels for 1.5-2 minutes per side.

m.   Put boiled bagels on baking sheets.

n.   Mix egg and water. Brush on bagels.

o.   Bake for 15-18 minutes until golden brown.

p.   Cool on sheet, then on wire rack.

q.   Enjoy with cream cheese, butter, or as you like!

Special Notes:

- For extra flavor, soak raisins in warm water with a splash of vanilla extract before adding to the dough.
- Try sprinkling some oats or seeds on top of the bagels after the egg wash for a crunchy texture.

5. Autumn Spice Bagels

These bagels bring the taste of fall to your breakfast table. Born in a small bakery in Vermont, they quickly became a local hit. Made with real pumpkin and warm spices, they're perfect for cool mornings. You'll love how they fill your kitchen with the scent of autumn.

Preparation Time: 30 minutes

Cooking Time: 30 minutes

Rise Time: 1 hour 10 minutes

Serving Size: 8 Bagels

Ingredients:

- 3 cups all-purpose flour, plus extra if needed
- 1 packet (¼ oz) active dry yeast
- 6 cups water
- 1 tbsp cornmeal
- 1 ½ tsp ground cinnamon
- ⅔ cup warm water (110°F)
- ¾ cup canned pumpkin
- ⅓ cup packed brown sugar
- ¾ tsp ground nutmeg
- ½ tsp ground allspice
- ½ tsp ground cloves
- 1 tsp white sugar
- 1 tsp salt
- Cooking spray

Instructions:

a. Mix yeast and warm water in a big bowl. Add pumpkin, brown sugar, and spices. Stir well.

b. Add flour slowly until you get a soft dough. Knead for 6-8 minutes by hand or use a mixer.

c. Put dough in a greased bowl. Cover with a damp towel. Let it rise in a warm spot for about an hour until it doubles.

d. Punch down the dough. Make 8 balls. Poke a hole in each to make bagel shapes. Let them rise for 10-15 minutes.

e. Boil water and sugar in a big pot. Flatten bagels a bit. Cook each side for 1½ minutes in the water. Dry on a towel.

f. Heat oven to 400°F. Spray a baking sheet and sprinkle with cornmeal. Place bagels 2 inches apart.

g. Bake for 25-30 minutes until done. Let cool before eating.

Special Notes:

- For extra flavor, brush bagels with melted butter mixed with maple syrup right after baking.
- Try adding a handful of chopped pecans to the dough for a nutty crunch. It'll make your bagels even more special.

6. Poppy Seed Bagels

These poppy seed bagels are a New York classic. They're chewy, tasty, and perfect for breakfast or lunch. You'll love the golden crust and soft inside. They're not hard to make at home, and you can add your favorite toppings. Give them a try!

Preparation Time: 1 hour 10 minutes

Cooking Time: 35 minutes

Serving Size: 12 bagels

Ingredients:

- 4 cups all-purpose flour
- 1&1/2 cups warm water
- 8 cups water, extra
- 2 tablespoons poppy seeds
- 1 tablespoon dried yeast
- 2 tablespoons sugar
- 2 teaspoons salt
- 1 egg yolk
- 1 tablespoon milk

Instructions:

a. Mix warm water, yeast, and 1 tablespoon sugar in a small bowl. Wait 5 minutes until it's bubbly.

b. In a big bowl, mix flour and salt. Make a hole in the middle. Pour in the yeast mix. Stir until it comes together.

c. Knead the dough on a floured surface for 10 minutes until smooth. Put it in a bowl, cover with plastic wrap, and let it rise for 30 minutes in a warm spot.

d. Heat oven to 350°F. In a large pot, bring extra water and remaining sugar to a boil, then lower to a simmer.

e. Oil a baking sheet. Split dough into 12 pieces. Roll each into a ball. Poke a hole in the middle with your finger. Flatten a bit. Let them sit for 10 minutes.

f.   Cook 4 bagels at a time in the simmering water for 3 minutes on each side. Take them out and put on the oiled sheet.

g.   Mix egg yolk and milk. Brush on bagels. Sprinkle with poppy seeds.

h.   Bake for 20 minutes until golden brown. Let cool before eating.

Special Notes:

- For extra chewy bagels, let the dough rise overnight in the fridge. This slow rise develops more flavor too.
- Try adding a tablespoon of barley malt syrup to the boiling water. It gives the bagels a nice shine and slight sweetness.

7. Garlicky Bagel Rings

These bagels are a New York classic with a garlic twist. They're chewy, flavorful, and perfect for breakfast or lunch. The roasted garlic adds a mellow, sweet flavor that garlic lovers will adore. You can make them at home and enjoy them fresh from the oven.

Preparation Time: 2 hours 50 minutes

Cooking Time: 20 minutes

Serving Size: 8 Bagels

Ingredients:

a. 4 cups all-purpose or bread flour

b. 1 small garlic bulb (about 8-10 cloves)

c. 2&1/4 teaspoons instant yeast 1&1/2 tablespoons sugar

d. 1&1/2 teaspoons salt

e. 1 egg (mixed with 1 teaspoon water for egg wash)

f. 1&1/2 tablespoons fennel seeds (optional, coarsely ground)

g. 1&1/4 cups warm water (plus extra 2 tablespoons if needed)

h. Extra fennel seeds (optional, for topping)

Instructions:

Make the garlic-fennel mix:

a. Heat oven to 400°F.

b. Cut the top off the garlic bulb, put in a small dish or foil.

c. Add oil, salt, and pepper. Wrap if using foil.

d. Bake for 40-45 minutes until brown and smell

e. Let it cool down.

While garlic cooks, toast fennel seeds in a dry pan. Grind them up.

Mash cooled garlic with ground fennel. Set aside.

Make the dough:

    a.   Mix flour, salt, and sugar in a big bowl.

    b.   Make a hole in the middle, add yeast.

    c.   Slowly add water while mixing.

    d.   When mostly mixed, add garlic-fennel mush.

    e.   Knead for 6-8 minutes until smooth.

    f.   If too dry, add water bit by bit. If too wet, add flour.

Let dough rise:

    a.   Shape into a ball, put in an oiled

    b.   Cover and let grow for an hour.

    c.   Punch it down, let it rest for 10 minutes.

Shape bagels:

    a.   Heat oven to 425°F. Boil water in a big pan.

    b.   Cut dough into 8 pieces.

    c.   Roll each piece into a ball.

    d.   Poke a hole in the middle, stretch it out.

Cook bagels:

    a.   Let the shaped bagels rest for 10 minutes.

    b.   Mix egg and water for egg wash.

    c.   Boil bagels for 1 minute each side.

    d.   Put on a baking sheet, brush with egg wash.

    e.   Add more fennel seeds on top if you want.

    f.   Bake for 20 minutes until golden brown.

Cool on a wire rack for 15-20 minutes before eating.

Special Notes:

- For extra garlicky flavor, mince a raw garlic clove and mix it into cream cheese as a spread.
- Try adding some dried herbs like rosemary or thyme to the dough for a flavor boost.

8. Whole Wheat Bagels

These whole wheat bagels are a New York breakfast staple. They're chewy, filling, and perfect for those busy mornings. Made with simple ingredients like whole wheat flour and maple syrup, these bagels will become your go-to breakfast. They're easy to make and taste great with your favorite toppings.

Preparation Time: 1 hour 35 minutes

Cooking Time: 25 minutes

Serving Size: 12 bagels

Ingredients:

- 4 cups whole wheat flour
- 1&1/2 cups warm water
- 4 teaspoons sugar
- 2&1/4 teaspoons active dry yeast
- 2 tablespoons pure maple syrup
- 2 teaspoons salt
- Optional: sesame seeds, poppy seeds or sea salt for topping

Instructions:

a. Mix warm water and yeast in a bowl. Let it sit until the yeast dissolves.

b. In a stand mixer bowl, put flour, syrup, salt, and sugar. Add the yeast mix.

c. Mix on low for 2 minutes until flour is mostly mixed in.

d. Switch to medium speed. Mix for 8-9 minutes until dough is smooth and elastic.

e. Shape dough into a ball. Put it in an oiled bowl, turning to coat. Cover with a damp towel and let rise in a warm spot for 20 minutes.

f. Heat oven to 425°F. Put a rack in the middle.

g. Boil water in a large pot, then lower heat to simmer. Keep covered.

h.   Get 3 baking sheets ready. Line 2 with parchment paper. Put a wire rack on the third.

i.   Cut dough into 12 equal pieces. Roll each into a ball. Poke a hole in the middle and stretch to make a ring.

j.   Boil bagels 3-4 at a time, 30 seconds each side. Drain on wire rack.

k.   Add toppings while bagels are wet.

l.   Put bagels on lined sheets, 1 inch apart. Bake for 15 minutes.

m.   Rotate pans and bake 8-10 more minutes until golden brown.

n.   Cool on a rack for at least 20 minutes.

o.   Store in a zip-lock bag or freeze sliced.

Special Notes:

- For extra chewy bagels, let the dough rise overnight in the fridge. This slow rise adds more flavor too.
- Try brushing the bagels with an egg wash before adding toppings. This helps the toppings stick better and gives the bagels a nice shine.

9. Blueberry Bagels

These bagels are a New York classic with a fruity twist. Blueberries add a burst of flavor and a pretty purple hue. They're chewy, slightly sweet, and perfect for breakfast or a snack. You'll love how the blueberries pop in every bite. Make a batch and watch them disappear!

Preparation Time: 2 hours 45 minutes (including rise time)

Cooking Time: 20 minutes Serving

Size: 8 Bagels

Ingredients:

- 3&1/2 cups bread flour, plus extra for dusting
- 1&1/4 cups fresh or frozen blueberries, thawed
- 1&1/2 teaspoons active dry yeast or instant yeast
- 2 tablespoons granulated sugar
- 1/2 teaspoon vanilla extract
- 1 teaspoon salt
- 1/2 cup + 1 Tablespoon lukewarm water (plus more if needed)

For Poaching:

- 2 quarts water
- 1 tablespoon honey or brown sugar

Instructions:

a. Cook blueberries in a small pot over low heat. Stir and mash until juicy. Let cool.

b. Mix water, yeast, and sugar in a big bowl. Wait 5-10 minutes if using active dry yeast.

c. Add flour, salt, cooked blueberries, and vanilla. Mix into a thick, slightly sticky dough. Add water if too dry.

d. Knead for 10 minutes by hand or with a mixer.

e. Shape into a ball, put in an oiled bowl, cover, and let rise until doubled.

f. Punch down dough and divide into 8 pieces. Shape each into a ball and rest for 5 minutes.

g. Make a hole in each ball with your thumbs, then stretch to form bagel shapes.

h. Place on a lined baking sheet and let rest for 30 minutes.

i. Heat oven to 425°F. Boil water in a large pot and add honey or sugar.

j. Boil bagels for 30 seconds on each side. Drain on a wire rack.

k. Bake for 20-25 minutes until golden brown. Turn the pan halfway if needed.

l. Cool on a rack for 30 minutes before slicing.

Special Notes:

- For extra flavor, try adding a teaspoon of lemon zest to the dough. It pairs well with the blueberries and adds a fresh kick.
- If you like a crunchier bagel, sprinkle some coarse sugar on top right before baking. It'll create a sweet, crispy crust.

10. Onion Bagels

These onion bagels are a New York favorite. They're chewy, tasty, and packed with onion flavor. People love them for breakfast or lunch. You can make them at home easily. They're great with cream cheese or as a sandwich base. Try them once, and you'll want to make them again.

Preparation Time: 1 hour 35 minutes

Cooking Time: 20 minutes

Serving size: 6 Bagels

Ingredients: Bagel dough:

- 2&1/2 cups all-purpose flour
- 1 tablespoon onion powder
- 1 cup warm water (about 115°F)
- 1&1/2 teaspoons active dry yeast (or 1/2 packet)
- 1 tablespoon sugar
- 1/2 tablespoon salt

Other:

- 1-2 tablespoons dried minced onion for topping
- 1/4 cup baking soda
- Water for boiling

Instructions:

a. Mix warm water, yeast, and sugar in a bowl. Wait 5 minutes until it's foamy.

b. In another bowl, mix salt, flour, and onion powder. Add this to the yeast mix. Stir well. Add more flour or water if needed to make a slightly sticky dough.

c. Knead the dough for 5-10 minutes until it springs back when you poke it.

d. Put the dough in a big bowl and cover with a wet cloth. Let it rise for about an hour until it doubles in size.

e. Punch the dough down and cut into 6 pieces. Form each piece into a ball, then poke a hole in the middle to make a bagel shape. Let them rise for 15 minutes more.

f. Get a baking sheet ready with parchment paper or non-stick spray.

g. In a deep pan, mix baking soda with enough water to float the bagels. Bring to a boil.

h. Boil the bagels 2-3 at a time, 1-2 minutes on each side. Take them out with a slotted spoon, drain on a towel, then put on the baking sheet.

i. Sprinkle dried minced onion on top of the bagels.

j. Bake at 400°F for 15-20 minutes until they're golden brown.

k. Let them cool for at least 5 minutes before eating.

Special Notes:

- For extra onion flavor, mix some finely chopped fresh onions into the dough before kneading.
- Try sprinkling some coarse salt on top with the dried onion for a flavor boost and nice crunch.

Savory Bagel Sandwiches

11. Steak and Egg Bagel Sandwich

This hearty sandwich comes from New York City. It's a favorite among busy workers and hungry folks. With juicy steak, gooey cheese, and a runny egg all tucked in a toasted bagel, it's a meal that'll keep you full till lunch. You'll love how quick and tasty it is.

Preparation Time: 5 minutes

Cooking Time: 20 minutes

Serving Size: 4 sandwiches

Ingredients:

- 8 slices cheddar cheese or white American cheese, thinly sliced
- 8 oz ribeye steak
- 4 bagels
- 4 eggs
- 1/4 white onion, thinly sliced
- 3 tbsp butter, divided
- Salt and black pepper
- Worcestershire sauce

Instructions:

a. Cut the steak into 4 thin pieces, about 1/2 inch thick and 4-5 inches wide. Sprinkle it with salt, pepper, and Worcestershire sauce. Set aside.

b. Melt 1 tbsp butter in a pan over medium heat. Add onions and cook for 9-12 minutes, stirring now and then, until soft and brown.

c. In another pan, melt 1 tbsp butter over medium-high heat. Cook steaks for about 1 minute on each side. Don't overcook. Set aside.

d. Melt the last 1 tbsp butter in a pan over medium-low heat. Crack in the eggs. Cook for 3 minutes, folding the whites to fit the bagel shape. Flip, add cheese on top, and cook 2-3 more minutes.

e.   While eggs cook, toast the bagels.

f.   Build your sandwich: Put cheese on both bagel halves. On the bottom half, add steak, onions, and the egg with cheese. Top with the other bagel half.

g.   Serve right away while it's hot.

Special Notes:

- For extra flavor, rub the steak with crushed garlic before cooking. It adds a nice kick without overpowering the meat.
- If you like your sandwich less messy, try scrambling the eggs instead of frying them. It's just as tasty but easier to eat on the go.

12. Sunrise Bagel Sandwich

This breakfast sandwich is a New York deli classic. It's quick, easy, and perfect for busy mornings. The combo of bagel, eggs, bacon, and cheese is sure to hit the spot. Whether you're rushing to work or nursing a headache, this sandwich will get you going.

Preparation Time: 10 minutes

Cooking Time: 5 minutes

Serving size: 1 sandwich

Ingredients:

- 2 slices American cheese
- 2 slices bacon, cooked
- 1 bagel (any type you like)
- 3 tablespoons butter, split
- 2 large eggs
- Salt and black pepper to taste

Instructions:

a. Cut the bagel in half. Spread 2 tablespoons of butter on the cut sides.

b. Heat a pan over medium heat. Toast the buttered bagel halves until golden. Set aside. If using a toaster, toast first, then butter.

c. Melt the last tablespoon of butter in the pan. Crack in both eggs. When the whites start to set, break the yolks and spread them around. Add salt and pepper.

d. Put the cheese and bacon on one egg. Flip the other egg on top of the bacon. Cook a bit longer to melt the cheese.

e. Move the egg stack to the bottom bagel half. Top with the other half.

f. Eat right away or wrap it up to go!

Special Notes:

- Secret flavor boost: Spread a thin layer of mayo on the bagel before adding the eggs. It adds a tangy kick that works great with the bacon and cheese.
- Veggie twist: Add a slice of tomato or some avocado to sneak in some extra nutrients and make the sandwich even more filling.

13. Turkey Avocado Bagel Bomb

This sandwich is a big hit in New York City delis. It's packed with turkey, avocado, and roasted tomatoes on a toasted everything bagel. The chipotle cream cheese adds a spicy kick. It's a quick and tasty meal that'll keep you full for hours.

Preparation Time: 20 minutes

Serving size: 2 sandwiches

Ingredients:

- 2 everything bagels, cut in half
- 1 large avocado, mashed
- 6 oz cream cheese, softened
- 6 oz thick-cut deli turkey breast
- 1 cup cherry tomatoes
- 1 tbsp adobo sauce
- 1 tsp lime juice
- 1/2 tsp salt
- 1/2 tsp black pepper
- 2/3 cup mixed greens
- 2 chipotle peppers, chopped (plus extra for more heat if desired)

Instructions:

a. Heat oven to 400°F. Spray a baking sheet with cooking spray.
b. Spread cherry tomatoes on the sheet. Roast for 10 minutes, flipping halfway. They should start to burst.
c. Mix cream cheese, adobo sauce, and 2 chopped chipotle peppers in a bowl. Set aside.
d. In another bowl, mix mashed avocado, lime juice, pepper, and salt.
e. Toast the bagels until golden.

f. Spread avocado mix on bottom halves of bagels. Spread chipotle cream cheese on top halves.

g. Layer turkey, greens, and roasted tomatoes on bottom halves. Add extra chopped chipotles if you like it spicier.

h. Put the top halves on and serve right away.

Special Notes:

- For extra crunch, try adding some crispy bacon bits or crushed tortilla chips on top of the turkey.
- If you're not a fan of spicy food, swap the chipotle cream cheese for a milder herb cream cheese. Mix in some chopped fresh basil or dill for a refreshing twist.

14. Eggy Bagel Stack

This quick sandwich comes from New York City's busy delis. It's a hit with busy folks who want a tasty, filling breakfast. The combo of bagel, eggs, cheese, and veggies makes it both yummy and healthy. You'll love how the creamy avocado balances the zesty pesto.

Preparation Time: 10 minutes

Cooking Time: 5 minutes

Serving Size: 1 sandwich

Ingredients:

- 1/2 cup arugula
- 1/2 avocado, sliced
- slice Havarti cheese (about 1 oz)
- large eggs
- Salt and pepper to taste
- Everything Bagel, toasted
- tablespoon pesto

Instructions:

a. Toast the bagel and spread pesto on both halves.

b. Mix eggs in a bowl. Add salt and pepper.

c. Cook eggs in a greased pan over medium-low heat until set.

d. Flip and cook the other side.

e. Put cheese on the eggs. Turn off heat and let it melt.

f. Stack your bagel: Bottom half, arugula, cheesy eggs, avocado slices, more salt and pepper, rest of arugula, top half.

g. Eat right away while it's hot!

Special Notes:

- Try toasting the bagel with a bit of garlic butter for extra flavor.
- For a protein boost, add a slice of turkey or bacon between the egg and avocado.

15. Veggie Bagel Bonanza

This veggie-packed bagel sandwich is a hit in New York delis. It's loaded with fresh veggies and tangy mustard. People love it for a quick lunch or light dinner. The mix of crunchy and soft textures makes it satisfying. It's easy to customize with your favorite toppings.

Preparation Time: 15 minutes

Cooking Time: 10 minutes

Serving size: 2 sandwiches

Ingredients:

- 6-8 thin slices tomato
- 2-4 thin slices red onion
- 2-4 large pickle slices
- 2-4 thin slices cucumber
- 2 everything bagels
- 1 cup spring mix
- 1/2 cup baby arugula
- 1/4 cup (2 oz) stone ground mustard
- 1/4 cup sliced roasted red pepper

Optional Toppings:

- Smoked paprika or cayenne pepper
- Plain or pickled jalapeños
- Hot or sweet pepper rings
- Spinach

Instructions:

a. If you like, lightly toast the bagels to soften them up.

b. Mix the spring mix and arugula in a bowl. Give them a rough chop.

c. Cut the bagels in half. Spread 1 tablespoon of mustard on each half, both top and bottom.

d. Put half of the chopped greens on the bottom half of each bagel.

e. Layer on the veggies: red peppers, cucumber, tomato, red onion, and pickle slices.

f. Put the top half of the bagel on.

g. Use a sharp knife to cut each sandwich in half.

h. Serve with chips on the side.

Special Notes:

- For extra crunch, try adding some alfalfa sprouts or thinly sliced radishes.
- If you're feeling adventurous, swap the stone ground mustard for a flavored hummus or avocado spread. It'll give the sandwich a whole new twist!

16. Chicken Salad Bagel Supreme

This Chicken Salad Bagel Supreme is a hit in New York delis. It's a quick lunch that packs a punch with juicy chicken, crisp veggies, and creamy dressing. Stuffed in a toasty bagel, it's a handheld meal that'll keep you full and happy. Perfect for picnics or busy workdays.

Preparation Time: 15 minutes

Cooking Time: 10 minutes

Serving Size: 4 sandwiches

Ingredients:

- 8 tomato slices
- 1 hard-boiled egg, peeled
- 1/2 medium sweet onion, quartered
- 1/2 cup salad dressing
- 1/2 teaspoon oregano
- 1/4 teaspoon salt
- 1/8 teaspoon pepper
- cup chopped cooked chicken breast
- stalks celery, cut in quarters
- lettuce leaves
- plain bagels

Instructions:

a. Toss chicken, celery, onion, salad dressing, oregano, salt, pepper, and egg in a food processor.

b. Pulse 4-5 times. Stop when everything's mixed and chopped rough.

c. Heat up your toaster and pop in the bagels. Toast them lightly.

d. Grab the bagel bottoms. Scoop a quarter of the chicken mix onto each one.

e. Add 2 tomato slices on top of the chicken.

f. Crown each with a lettuce leaf.

g. Cap it off with the bagel tops.

h. Enjoy your Crunchy Cluck Stack!

Special Notes:

- Secret crunch boost: Mix in a handful of chopped walnuts or sliced water chestnuts with the chicken salad for extra texture.
- Flavor twist: Try swapping the plain bagels for everything bagels. The added seasoning gives a tasty kick to your sandwich.

17. Smoked Salmon Bagel Stack

This New York-inspired sandwich is a favorite for brunch or light meals. It's a mix of smoky salmon, creamy cheese, and tangy pickles on a chewy bagel. People love it for its fresh taste and easy prep. It's perfect for those who want a quick, tasty bite.

Preparation Time: 15 minutes

Serving size: 4 sandwiches

Ingredients: For the bagel:

- 5 oz cream cheese
- 4 bagels, cut in half and toasted
- 7 oz sustainable smoked salmon
- 1-2 tbsp capers, rinsed and drained
- Few sprigs fresh dill (optional)

For the quick-pickled cucumber and red onion:

- 1 cucumber, peeled into long strips
- 1 tbsp sugar
- 1 tsp salt
- 1 tsp lemon zest
- 1/2 small red onion, thinly sliced
- Small handful dill, finely chopped (or parsley if you don't like dill)
- 1/4 cup apple cider vinegar (or any vinegar you have)

Instructions:

a. Mix vinegar, sugar, salt, lemon zest, and chopped dill in a bowl.

b. Add cucumber strips and onion slices to the mix. Let it sit for at least 15 minutes.

c. Toast the bagel halves.

d. Spread cream cheese on the bottom half of each bagel.

e. Layer smoked salmon on top of the cream cheese.

f. Sprinkle capers over the salmon.

g. Add a heap of pickled veggies on top.

h. Season with black pepper and add dill sprigs if you want.

i. Put the top half of the bagel on.

j. Cut each bagel in half and serve with lemon wedges.

Special Notes:

- Try adding a thin slice of ripe avocado for extra creaminess.
- For a twist, mix some horseradish into the cream cheese for a spicy kick.

18. Honey Apple Bagel Bonanza

This sandwich was born in a New York deli. It's a hit with busy folks who want something tasty and quick. The mix of sweet and salty flavors will wake up your taste buds. It's perfect for those mornings when you need a boost to start your day right.

Preparation Time: 5 minutes

Cooking Time: 10 minutes

Serving Size: 2 sandwiches

Ingredients:

- 2-4 slices prosciutto
- 2 sesame bagels
- 1/2 Granny Smith apple
- 1/4 cup cream cheese
- 2 tablespoons honey
- 1 cup arugula

Instructions:

a. Cut the bagels in half and pop them in the toaster.

b. While the bagels are toasting, mix the cream cheese and honey in a small bowl.

c. Slice the apple thinly.

d. Once the bagels are toasted, spread the honey cream cheese on the bottom half of each bagel.

e. Layer on the apple slices, then the prosciutto, and top with a handful of arugula.

f. Put the top half of the bagel on and press down gently.

g. Cut each sandwich in half and serve right away.

Special Notes:

- Try warming the prosciutto in a pan for 30 seconds before adding it to the sandwich. This brings out its flavor and makes it slightly crispy.
- For a tangy twist, add a squeeze of lemon juice to the arugula before putting it on the sandwich. This brightens up the flavors and adds a nice zing.

19. Toasted Bagel Delight

This sandwich was born in a New York deli. It's a hit with busy folks who want something tasty and filling. Ham, cheese, and spinach team up inside a warm bagel. It's easy to make and will keep you full till lunch. You'll love how the melted cheese oozes with every bite.

Preparation Time: 5 minutes

Cooking Time: 20 minutes

Serving Size: 1 sandwich

Ingredients:

- 1 large bagel
- 2 slices Swiss cheese
- 2-4 thin slices ham
- 2 teaspoons mayonnaise
- 2 teaspoons Dijon mustard
- 1/4 teaspoon Worcestershire sauce
- 1/4 cup fresh spinach, loosely packed
- 1/4 teaspoon poppy seeds
- teaspoon butter, melted

Instructions:

a. Turn on your oven. Set it to 350°F.

b. Mix up your spread. Put mayonnaise, Dijon mustard, and Worcestershire sauce in a small bowl. Stir them together.

c. Get your bagel ready. Cut it in half. Spread the mayo mix on both inside parts.

d. Stack your sandwich. Start with spinach. Then add ham and cheese. Keep adding until you use it all up. Close the bagel.

e. Make the topping. Mix melted butter and poppy seeds in a small bowl. Brush this on top of the closed bagel.

f. Wrap it up. Put the bagel on a big piece of foil. Fold the foil around it so it's all covered.

g. Bake time! Put the wrapped bagel in the oven for 15-20 minutes. It's done when it's warm and the cheese is melty.

h. Take it out and cut it in half. Now eat and enjoy!

Special Notes:

- Secret flavor boost: Add a slice of ripe tomato before baking. It adds a fresh, juicy kick to the sandwich.
- Crispy trick: Open the foil for the last 2 minutes of baking. This makes the bagel top extra crispy and golden.

20. Tuna Twist Bagel Bonanza

This quick and easy tuna bagel sandwich is a lunchtime favorite. Born in New York delis, it's now loved worldwide. With creamy tuna mix and soft bagels, it's a tasty meal you'll want again and again. Perfect for busy days or lazy weekends.

Preparation Time: 10 minutes

Serving Size: 3 sandwiches

Ingredients:

- 3 bagels
- 1/2 cup mayonnaise
- 2 cans (5 oz each) tuna, drained
- 1/2 to 1 celery stalk, finely chopped (optional)

Instructions:

a. Put the tuna in a bowl. Add the mayonnaise.
b. Use a fork to mix everything. Break the tuna into small bits as you stir.
c. If you want, chop up some celery and add it to the mix. Stir it in.
d. Cut your bagels in half.
e. Scoop the tuna mix onto the bagel halves.
f. Put the top half of the bagel on and enjoy your sandwich!

Special Notes:

- Try adding a squeeze of lemon juice to the tuna mix. It gives a fresh, zingy taste that wakes up your taste buds.
- For a crunchy twist, toast the bagels lightly before adding the tuna. The mix of soft tuna and crispy bagel is a real treat for your mouth!

Sweet Bagel Treats

21. Chocolate Chip Bagels

These bagels are a sweet twist on the classic New York staple. Mixing chocolate chips into the dough makes them extra yummy. They're great for breakfast or a snack. You'll love how the chocolate melts a bit when you toast them. They're not hard to make and taste way better than store-bought ones.

Preparation Time: 45 minutes

Cooking Time: 20 minutes

Serving Size: 6 bagels

Ingredients:

- 2&1/2 cups bread flour
- 1/2 teaspoon instant dry yeast
- 1/4 cup chocolate chips
- 1 cup lukewarm water
- 1 tablespoon honey (for water bath)
- 1 tablespoon brown sugar
- 1 teaspoon salt
- 1 egg (for egg wash, optional)

Instructions:

a. Mix flour, sugar, yeast, and salt in a big bowl. Add water and mix for 7-8 minutes. The dough will be sticky at first.

b. Move the dough to a floured surface. Knead until it's smooth.

c. Cut the dough into 6 pieces. Push chocolate chips into each piece. Fold the dough over any chips you can see and pinch it closed.

d. Cover the dough and let it sit for 30 minutes. It'll puff up a little.

e. Boil water in a big pot. Add honey. Drop in 2 bagels at a time. Let them float for about 15 seconds, flipping once.

f. Take out the bagels with a slotted spoon. Put them on a baking sheet.

g. If you want, brush them with beaten egg.

h. Bake at 375°F for about 20 minutes. They should be golden brown and feel firm.

i. Eat them warm with your favorite toppings.

Special Notes:

- For extra flavor, try adding a pinch of cinnamon to the dough. It goes great with chocolate!
- If you like your bagels chewier, let them float in the boiling water for up to 30 seconds instead of 15.

22. Sweet Sunrise Bagel

This quick and easy breakfast treat combines creamy peanut butter, smooth Nutella, and fresh banana slices on a toasted bagel. It's a popular morning pick-me-up in busy cafes. You'll love how the flavors blend together, giving you a tasty start to your day.

Preparation Time: 5 minutes

Cooking Time: 5 minutes

Serving Size: 2 sandwiches

Ingredients:

- 2 tablespoons Nutella
- 2 plain bagels
- 2 tablespoons peanut butter
- 1 whole banana, sliced
- Chocolate puff pearls for decoration (optional)

Instructions:

a. Mix the peanut butter and Nutella in a small bowl until well combined. Set aside.

b. Cut the bagels in half and toast them until golden brown.

c. Spread the peanut butter-Nutella mixture evenly on all bagel halves.

d. Top each bagel half with banana slices.

e. If desired, sprinkle chocolate puff pearls over the banana slices for extra crunch and flavor.

f. Serve immediately and enjoy your Sweet Sunrise Bagel!

Special Notes:

- For a warm, gooey treat, try assembling the bagel and then toasting it in a panini press or on a griddle. The heat will melt the spread and warm the bananas, creating a delightful texture contrast.
- Experiment with different nut butters like almond or cashew butter for varied flavors. You can also try adding a sprinkle of cinnamon or a drizzle of honey for extra sweetness.

23. Strawberry Cream Cheese Bagel Bliss

This quick and easy bagel sandwich is a New York classic. It's a go-to breakfast for many city dwellers. The combo of cream cheese and fresh strawberries on a toasted bagel is simple but so good. You'll love how the sweet honey brings it all together.

Preparation Time: 5 minutes

Cooking Time: 5 minutes

Serving size: 2 sandwiches

Ingredients:

- 4 oz low fat cream cheese
- 2 bagels
- 1 cup strawberries, sliced
- 1 tbsp honey

Instructions:

a. Cut the bagels in half.

b. Toast the bagel halves until they're golden brown.

c. Spread cream cheese on each bagel half.

d. Put lots of sliced strawberries on top of the cream cheese.

e. Drizzle honey over the strawberries.

f. Eat right away while it's still warm.

Special Notes:

- Try warming the honey a bit before drizzling. It'll spread easier and soak into the bagel more.
- For a twist, add a sprinkle of cinnamon or a few leaves of fresh mint on top. It'll give your bagel an extra pop of flavor.

24. Bagel French Toast Surprise

This recipe takes plain bagels and turns them into a sweet breakfast treat. It's a fun twist on regular French toast that's quick to make. People love it because it's easy and tastes great. You can use any kind of bagel you like, but cinnamon raisin works really well.

Preparation Time: 5 minutes

Cooking Time: 10 minutes

Serving Size: 2 sandwiches

Ingredients:

- 2 bagels
- 2 large eggs
- 1/2 cup milk
- 1/4 teaspoon ground cinnamon
- 1 teaspoon vanilla extract
- 1 pinch of salt
- 1 tablespoon unsalted butter

Instructions:

a. Grab a mixing bowl and crack the eggs into it. Pour in the milk, then add the cinnamon, vanilla, and a pinch of salt. Mix everything together well with a whisk or fork.

b. Cut your bagels in half. Dip each piece into the egg mixture.

c. Let them soak for about 30 seconds on each side so they get nice and eggy.

d. Put a pan on the stove and turn the heat to medium. Add the butter and let it melt.

e. Once the butter melted, put the soaked bagel pieces in the pan.

f. Cook them for a few minutes on each side until they turn golden brown.

g. Take the bagels out of the pan and put them on plates.

h. Add your favorite toppings like maple syrup, powdered sugar, or fresh berries.

i. Dig in and enjoy your Bagel French Toast Surprise!

Special Notes:

- Try using stale bagels for this recipe. They soak up the egg mixture better and get extra crispy when cooked.

- For a savory twist, skip the cinnamon and vanilla. Instead, add a pinch of garlic powder and some grated cheese to the egg mixture. Top with a fried egg for a hearty breakfast sandwich.

25. Bagel with Peanut Butter and Jelly

This sandwich is a tasty twist on the classic PB&J. It's a favorite in New York City delis. Everything bagel adds a nice crunch and flavor. You'll love how the warm, toasted bagel melts the peanut butter. It's quick to make and perfect for breakfast or lunch.

Preparation Time: 15 minutes

Cooking Time: 15 minutes

Serving size: 2 sandwiches

Ingredients:

For the PB&J Bagels:

- 2 everything bagels
- 4 tablespoons peanut butter
- 2 tablespoons unsalted butter
- 4 tablespoons jelly or marmalade of choice

For the Homemade Strawberry Jelly (optional):

- 1 tablespoon lemon juice
- 1 teaspoon cornstarch
- 1 cup strawberries, chopped
- 1/4 cup brown sugar

Instructions:

a. If making homemade jelly, mix strawberries, brown sugar, lemon juice, and cornstarch in a pot. Cook until thick. Cool and store in the fridge.

b. Melt butter in a skillet over medium heat.

c. Cut bagels in half and toast them in the skillet. Press down with a spatula.

d. Take bagels out of the skillet and cut each half into two pieces.

e. Spread peanut butter on four bagel pieces. Add jelly on top.

f. Put the other four bagel pieces on top to make sandwiches.

g. Eat and enjoy!

Special Notes:

- Try grilling the bagel with butter on both sides for extra crispiness. It'll make the peanut butter extra melty and delicious.

- For a fun twist, mix a little honey into your peanut butter before spreading. It adds a sweet touch that goes great with the salty everything bagel.

36. Peachy Cream Bagel Bliss

This bagel treat comes from a New York deli. It's a hit with locals and tourists. The mix of sweet peaches, creamy cheese, and a touch of honey makes it stand out. You'll love how the flavors work together. It's perfect for breakfast or a quick snack.

Preparation Time: 15 minutes

Cooking Time: 5 minutes

Serving Size: 4

Ingredients:

- 4 small ripe peaches
- 4 teaspoons honey
- 8 oz cream cheese or ricotta cheese
- 4 bagels (any kind you like)
- 2 sprigs fresh thyme

Instructions:

a. Toast your bagels how you like them.

b. Spread cream cheese on each bagel half.

c. Wash and slice the peaches.

d. Put peach slices on top of the cream cheese.

e. Drizzle honey over the peaches.

f. Pull thyme leaves off the sprigs and sprinkle them on top.

g. Eat and enjoy your tasty bagel!

Special Notes:

- For extra crunch, try toasting some sliced almonds and sprinkling them on top.
- If peaches aren't in season, you can use canned peaches. Just drain them well before using.

27. Blueberry Bagel Bliss

This tasty breakfast treat comes from New York City. It's a twist on the classic bagel and cream cheese. The sweet blueberry sauce and creamy mascarpone make it extra yummy. It's quick to make and perfect for busy mornings or weekend brunches.

Preparation Time: 10 minutes

Cooking Time: 10 minutes

Serving Size: 2 sandwiches

Ingredients:

- 2 pretzel bagels or plain bagels
- 1/4 teaspoon fresh lemon juice
- 1 teaspoon water
- 1 teaspoon granulated sugar
- 1 teaspoon lemon zest
- 1/4 cup blueberries
- 2 tablespoons mascarpone cheese

Instructions:

a. Toast the bagels until they're nice and brown.

b. In a small pot, mix the blueberries, sugar, and water. Cook on medium-high heat.

c. Keep cooking until the sugar melts and the blueberries start to pop. The liquid should turn purple. This takes about 1-2 minutes.

d. Take the pot off the heat. Add the lemon juice and stir everything together. Set it aside.

e. Spread the mascarpone cheese on your toasted bagels.

f. Spoon the blueberry mix on top of the mascarpone.

g. Sprinkle the lemon zest over everything.

h. Eat and enjoy your tasty bagel!

Special Notes:

- For extra flavor, try adding a pinch of cinnamon to the blueberry mix while cooking.
- If you're in a hurry, you can use store-bought blueberry jam instead of making the compote. Just warm it up a bit before spreading.

28. Sweet & Savory Bagel Stack

This tasty sandwich was born in a New York deli. It's a hit with busy folks who want something quick and yummy. The main stars are ricotta, figs, and a crunchy sesame snap. You'll love how the sweet and salty flavors mix together. It's perfect for breakfast or a snack.

Preparation Time: 5 minutes

Cooking Time: 5 minutes

Serving Size: 1 sandwich

Ingredients:

- 1/4 cup ricotta cheese
- 1 fig, sliced
- 1 teaspoon honey
- 1 sesame snap
- 1 teaspoon blackcurrant jam
- 1 cinnamon raisin bagel, toasted (or 2 slices fruit bread)

Instructions:

a. In a small bowl, mix the ricotta cheese with honey until smooth.

b. Cut the toasted bagel in half (or use 2 slices of fruit bread).

c. Spread the ricotta mixture evenly on both cut sides of the bagel.

d. On one half of the bagel, spread the blackcurrant jam.

e. Place the sliced fig on top of the jam.

f. Break the sesame snap into small pieces and sprinkle over the fig slices.

g. Close the sandwich by placing the other bagel half on top, ricotta side down.

h. Press gently to make sure everything sticks together.

i. Serve right away and enjoy your tasty creation!

Special Notes:

- Try warming the fig slices in the microwave for 10 seconds before adding them to the sandwich. This makes them extra soft and sweet.
- If you're out of sesame snaps, try crushing some plain sesame seeds and mixing them with a bit of honey. Drizzle this over the figs for a similar crunchy-sweet effect.

29. Blueberry Bliss Bagel

This sweet and tangy breakfast treat comes from New York City. It's a hit among busy folks who want a quick, tasty morning meal. The combo of lemon curd, fresh berries, and whipped cream on a toasted bagel is sure to wake up your taste buds. You'll love how easy it is to make!

Preparation Time: 10 minutes

Serving size: 1 sandwich

Ingredients:

- 1 plain bagel
- 1 cup blueberries
- 1 teaspoon vanilla extract
- 1 cup heavy cream
- 1 tablespoon powdered sugar
- 1/2 cup lemon curd
- Extra blueberries for topping

Instructions:

a. Chop the blueberries: Toss 1 cup of blueberries into a food processor or blender. Give them a quick buzz until they're roughly chopped.

b. Make the cream: In a bowl, mix the heavy cream, powdered sugar, and vanilla. Whip it up until it's fluffy. Gently fold in the chopped blueberries.

c. Prep the bagel: Cut the bagel in half and pop it in the toaster. Toast until it's golden and crispy.

d. Assemble: Spread a thick layer of lemon curd on both bagel halves. Top with a big spoonful of the blueberry cream mixture.

e. Finish it off: Sprinkle some whole blueberries on top for extra flavor and looks.

Special Notes:

- For a zingy twist, add a pinch of lemon zest to the whipped cream mixture. It'll make the flavors pop even more!
- If you're feeling fancy, try using different types of berries like raspberries or blackberries. Mix them with the blueberries for a colorful and tasty surprise.

30. Apple Cinnamon Bagel

This tasty breakfast sandwich is a New York favorite. It's quick, easy, and perfect for busy mornings. The apple and cinnamon spread adds a sweet twist to the classic bagel. You'll love how the crisp apple slices contrast with the creamy cheese. It's a simple yet satisfying way to start your day.

Preparation Time: 15 minutes

Cooking Time: 10 minutes

Serving Size: 2 sandwiches

Ingredients:

- 4 oz whipped cream cheese 2 bagels, sliced in half and toasted
- 4 tbsp Cinnamon Apple Jelly Spread
- 1 apple, cored and cut into 1/8-inch-thick slices

Instructions:

a. Mix the cream cheese and Cinnamon Apple Jelly in a bowl until well combined.
b. Spread this mixture on the bottom half of each toasted bagel.
c. Place apple slices on top of the cream cheese mixture.
d. Put the top half of the bagel on the apple slices.
e. Serve and enjoy your fruity bagel sandwich!

Special Notes:

- For extra crunch, try toasting the bagel with a bit of butter before adding the spread.
- If you're feeling adventurous, sprinkle a pinch of sea salt on the apple slices. It brings out the sweetness and adds a surprising flavor twist!

Conclusion

Now that you've tried these bagel recipes, you're well on your way to becoming a bagel expert. Remember, practice makes perfect. Don't worry if your first few attempts aren't exactly like the bagels from your favorite New York deli. With time and experience, you'll develop a feel for the dough and learn how to shape and boil bagels to perfection.

Feel free to experiment with different flavors and toppings. Try mixing in new ingredients or creating your own unique bagel sandwiches. The world of bagels is full of possibilities, and now you have the skills to explore it.

Homemade bagels are more than just food - they're a way to bring people together. Share your creations with family and friends, or surprise someone with a batch of freshly baked bagels. There's nothing quite like the smell of bagels baking in the oven to make a house feel like home.

We hope this cookbook has inspired you to make bagels a regular part of your baking routine. Whether you're whipping up a quick breakfast sandwich or preparing for a big brunch, these recipes will serve you well.

Remember, the key to great bagels is using quality ingredients and giving the dough the time it needs to develop flavor. Be patient, have fun, and enjoy the process as much as the end result.

Thank you for joining us on this bagel-making journey. Here's to many delicious breakfasts, lunches, and snacks in your future!

My Words

I cannot express enough how grateful I am for your decision to purchase my book. It is a humbling feeling to know that people are interested in learning from my experiences and the content that I have created. Being a writer has allowed me to share my knowledge and skills with others, and it is truly an honor to have you choose my book out of the multitude of books available on the market.

Your choice to invest in my book is incredibly special to me, and I am confident that the content you will find within its pages will prove to be valuable and insightful. It is my sincere hope that you will learn a great deal from the knowledge I have shared and that it will positively impact your life in some way.

After reading the book, I kindly request that you leave feedback, no matter how small. As a writer, I am always looking to improve and provide better content to my readers. Your feedback will be an invaluable source of information, and I will take it into consideration when creating future books. It is my goal to create content that my readers love and find helpful, and your input will play an important role in helping me achieve that.

Once again, I would like to express my gratitude for your support and for choosing my book. Your investment in my work means the world to me, and I am honored to have the opportunity to share my knowledge with you. Your feedback and support will be greatly appreciated and will help me to continue creating meaningful and valuable content for readers like you.

Kind regards,

Alex Aton

Printed in Dunstable, United Kingdom

74485941R00057